Praise for *How to Save the World*

"I wish I had this during my twenty-five-year tenure as a Financial Advisor. It would have been valuable in educating my clients about evaluating and prioritizing their charitable giving. I hope other Financial Advisors take a look at this publication."

—Sara Mushlitz, Wells Fargo, Senior Financial Advisor, retired

"*How To Save The World* spotlights how to help the millions of desperate people in the world. Two decades ago, I co-authored a book with the subtitle How the World Is Changed. The world is changed in part by people directing their resources where those in need can be helped. This book tells you how to do that strategically, effectively, and personally. If everyone followed the guidance here, the lives of millions could be improved."

—Michael Quinn Patton, Founder and Director, Utilization-Focused Evaluation

"With easy humor and heartfelt insight, Steve has written a thoughtful book that has inspired me to think more broadly and deeply about the organizations I choose to support. He brings broad knowledge and deep experience to the exploration of the effective non-profit organization. A great resource!"

—Tamra Nelson, Neighbor

"It's high time that the public is given an understanding of how peoples' own lives can help change the world and tools to engage and support nonprofits whose missions fit with their own interests and values."

—Emil W. Angelica, Amherst H. Wilder Foundation, retired; Community Consulting Group, Consultant

"Finally, a recipe with realistic ingredients that will help non-profits such as mine acquire "for real" guidance. Based upon years of experience and understanding of philanthropic culture, Steven Mayer has unselfishly made it plain and simple for us to follow. Onward!"

—Rose McGee, President and Founder of Sweet Potato Comfort Pie: a catalyst for caring and building community

"Every CPA should read this if they want to be of more help to their charitably inclined clients."

—Barry Rubin, retired CPA

"Congratulations for distilling the wisdom you've gained from a life of activism with a study of practices and strategies that make for effective nonprofits. You've created a compact, crisply written guidebook with tools and tips we donors can use—and nonprofits can look to as well—and reminded us of the values of honesty, trust, empathy, humility, respect, and dignity we must cultivate in our collective efforts to make the world a better place."

—Ron Kroese, Cofounder, Land Stewardship Project; Program Officer, McKnight Foundation Environment Program, retired

"Congratulations on this truly extraordinary and much-needed book. While I have long admired your writing and deep thinking about nonprofit and philanthropic organizations, I am in awe of this magnificent guide. Your ability to use inviting and very understandable language to explain important ideas, concepts, and insights about the sector is simply remarkable and brilliant. How to Save the World—a how-to book for making choices—deserves a vast audience."

—Arthur T. Himmelman, University of Minnesota Hubert H. Humphrey Institute Senior Fellow, retired; The McKnight Foundation, Senior Program Officer, retired

"Can one person really save the world? Well maybe not alone, but once again Steven Mayer shows us that we are all part of a larger community, and our collective actions can and DO make a difference. A great read for any donor who wants to leave the world a better place."

—Steve Joul, President and CEO, CommunityGiving.org

How To Save The World

Evaluating Your Choices

When to Say Yes to
Requests to Donate Now

Steven E. Mayer, Ph.D.

Wisdom Editions

Minneapolis

**Wisdom
Editions**

Minneapolis

FIRST EDITION September 2023

How to Save the World: Evaluating Your Choices
Copyright 2023 by Effective Communities LLC
All rights reserved.

10 9 8 7 6 5 4 3 2 1

ISBN: 978-1-962834-00-1

Cover and interior design: Nancy Hope

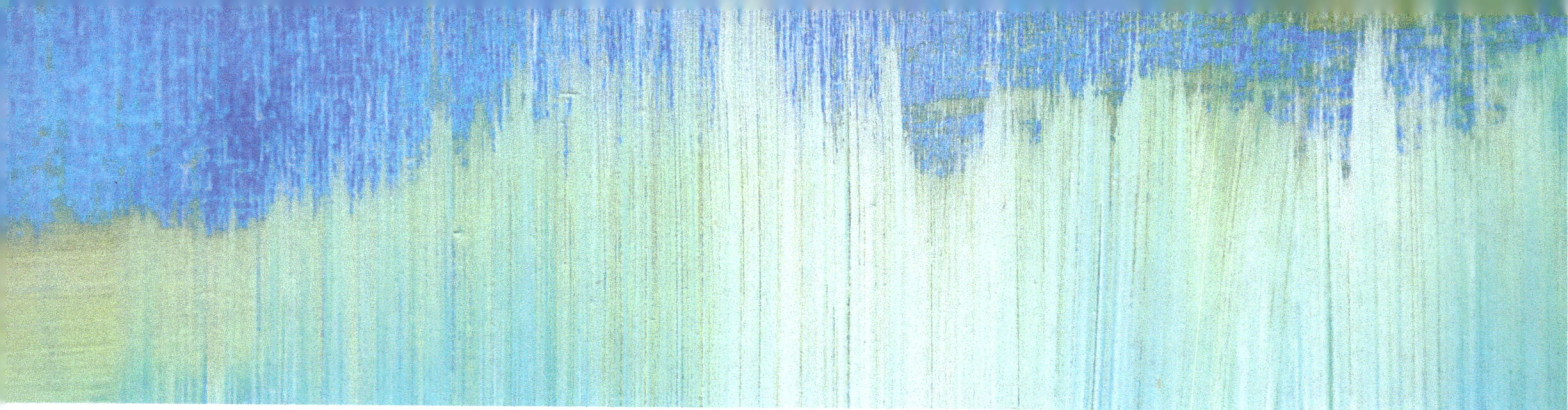

I dedicate this book to my father,
Paul A. Mayer, who once said to me,
"The last thing I want is for you to become
one of those save-the-world types."

Contents

Introduction

- The world is in an uproar. There's breakdown, dysfunction, and despair. It's easy to feel helpless. Most of us wish we knew how to help.

- But alongside the breakdown and dysfunction, there's also good work going on.

- All communities and people have assets with which to build.

- But it's an uphill battle. The stories of Don Quixote and Sisyphus seem to apply.

- We probably can't save the world by ourselves, though we each bring something. One thing's for sure: it will require people's participation.

- You—and everyone else—have assets that can be brought to the task of "saving the world," and I don't mean just money, prayers, and good wishes.

- The focus of this book is to help you make informed choices from among all the opportunities presented to you daily.

- Bringing a career's experience, I hope to show how you can direct your resources to help organizations that deal with issues you care about – to help them get to the next level of world-saving effectiveness.

Focus of this book

No matter the issue, it will take money, talent, and time—
as well as some good decisions—to create change. If big problems
were easy to solve, they'd have been solved already.

- Philanthropic institutions and governments may have money and/or talent, but it's not clear they know what they're doing. Or more charitably, it's not clear they act on what they know. But they certainly act like they have all the time in the world. Not good enough!

- So this book is directed to you, an obviously thoughtful person if you've read this far. You know that money can be used strategically to make good things happen—good things that together can help Save the World.

- What can You do to save the world? Take a good look, a closer look, at all those solicitations you get in your mail, your phone, your laptop, your eyeballs on the street. The folks they're from are happy to tell you how you can help. But you probably can't say Yes to all of them, even if you wanted to.

- In this book we focus on the role of nonprofit organizations, the big ones and perhaps even more, the smaller ones. We focus on the useful roles they can play, and how they work to achieve their mission.

- And we focus on the useful roles You can play in their support.

Almost everything I present in this little book is supported by the professional work I've done over the years, as can be found on the website of my own Effective Communities Project.

I'm talking to You

My career has been spent working primarily with nonprofit organizations, community foundations, and private foundations—always with the intention to learn how their work can be made more effective in bringing their missions to life.

But this time I'm talking to You.

- If you have ever donated to your alma mater, your places of worship, the hospital that saved you or your best friend's child from disaster, the places that gave you positive experiences growing up or now as an adult out of a wish to "give back."

- If you've ever bought Girl Scout cookies, tickets to the theater, museum, concert hall, or community events center, or sent money to support families in distress.

- If you've ever volunteered at a food pantry, community clean-up, disaster relief center, senior living center, animal shelter, or literacy program – and felt good for doing it but also wondered if there isn't a better way.

- If you've served on the Board of a nonprofit organization and seen what it's like to govern an effort to do good for individuals, their communities, and the social systems we all depend on – and seen the challenge of presenting the organization in the best light possible in the struggle to raise the money needed to sustain operations and grow its impact.

- If you've been favored in life enough to have your taxes done by an accountant, pay someone for financial advice, or have a Last Will in which you name a few charities as beneficiaries.

- If you get a ton of solicitations in the mail, more than you can keep up with, more than you can sort with confidence into 3 piles: Donate Now, Maybe Later, and No Thanks.

If you see yourself in these descriptions, I'm talking to You. And I salute you!

This book intends to help You as an individual evaluate those requests to Donate Now and prioritize your choices with greater confidence.

It also intends to help nonprofit organizations present themselves with greater pride of accomplishment and clarity of presentation, philanthropic advisors looking for better ways to understand and shape their clients' preferences, and foundation staff wanting to sharpen their understanding of principles for judging merit and advancing their grantees to the next level of effectiveness.

About the author

- Steven E. Mayer, Ph.D.
- Chief Strategist, Effective Communities Project
- I've worked for years on this stuff—academia, frontlines, evaluating, consulting, teaching.
- Much of my work is posted to EffectiveCommunities.com

Chapter 1
Saving the world:
The work of nonprofit organizations

Who does what?

Question: Considering the current state of the world, anyone can reasonably ask...

- Who did this?
- And who's going to do what to make it better?

Answers: all the below

- Individuals and families—those that care and those that don't;
- Communities—and the loose-to-strong networks they form;
- Government agencies—from very local to national and beyond;
- Private enterprise—from Main Street to global and in-between;
- Nonprofit organizations—working at levels from your family, to your neighborhood, county, state, national, and global.

For better and for worse, you yourself are already participating, knowingly or not, in all five of those arenas.

Tip: Because you play a role in each of those arenas, you're in a good position to make the world a better place.

Your role

Can you save the world just by yourself? Maybe, maybe not.

But for sure, many legitimate and valuable efforts are made solo. Our culture – everyone's culture – is full of stories of the power of human beings to make a difference.

- For example, extending respect along with your wish to understand can go amazingly far in building trust. They help to restore dignity, strength, and inspiration to those who need it. Which is pretty much everyone. If we all felt dignity, strength, and inspiration, we can consider the world saved.

- With trust, relationships can be built. From relationships can spring partnerships, and from partnerships can spring momentum for constructive change.

- Just showing up and joining with others to make something good happen can create innovation and launch untold progress.

- You have all the permission in the world to be a party to that.

And that can be your introduction to the wonderful world of nonprofit organizations, people on a mission already working on the whole range of challenging social problems.

- Your mailbox is probably full of their appeals for your help. They're everywhere, with missions from the divine to the mundane to the highly practical – intending to upgrade the quality of our lives.

You might be thinking of saying Yes to these appeals.

- But you probably can't say Yes to everyone who asks, or even to everyone you'd like to help. You have the authority to make choices about what to say Yes to.

- In this book we're wanting to help you inform that choice.

What do you care about?

Below, in all the many arenas of worldly affairs, there's great stress – in some places more than others. There's also great work going on – also in some places more than others.

- The first basics: air, water, and food – the essential ingredients to support human life.

- Safety – from disaster, accidents, illness, and harm.

- Shelter – a warm safe place, hopefully with loved ones.

- Education & skills – using hands, head, and heart creatively and usefully.

- Arts & culture – ways to express oneself, with creativity and meaning, rooted in the past and present of your culture, and others' too.

- Justice – experiencing fairness, responsibility, and dignity for all (as well as for you).

- Faith, spirit, generosity, self–actualization – what distinguishes humans from beasts.

You may recognize this list as Maslow's Hierarchy of Needs. One can speak of Needs, but on the flip side one can speak of Strengths or Assets, which is what you build with. More on this distinction later.

Tip: You may also see bits of your own life, past and present, here and there, and begin to identify interests or causes you may want to support.

The work of nonprofit organizations

One key to this book is its focus on nonprofit organizations and their missions as central to the work of saving the world.

- It's the mission of a nonprofit to contribute to the work of saving the world. The US Internal Revenue Service may choose to recognize an organization's mission as "charitable" and confer it with tax–exempt status.

- Like a business, a nonprofit takes in resources, but unlike a business its product or service intends to advance a social or charitable purpose—its mission.

- A nonprofit takes in resources and produces work that intends to advance a social or charitable purpose—ts mission. The nonprofit may make money (a net gain of revenue over expenses, roughly speaking) but this excess can be used only to serve the mission of the organization; it cannot be used for private gain.

- While any individual or organization, from families to government agencies to private business can be "socially–concerned," only nonprofit organizations make it their sole purpose

Tip: The world of nonprofits is big with diverse interests, and not easy to understand. A smart donor learns this world, its purposes and its ways of operating.

Nonprofit mission statements

Every nonprofit organization creates its unique mission, or in the eyes of the IRS, its "charitable purpose."

■ This is usually expressed as a "mission statement" and can typically be seen on its website (under About), in its founding papers, annual report, and sometimes its public appeals for support. These statements vary in clarity and sophistication, depending on the number of consultants involved in its creation.

■ A mission statement typically stakes out the geographic area or communities the community serves, and the charitable benefits it intends to provide, whether in education, justice, safety, etc.

■ If the mission statement looks like it was designed by committee, it probably was and there's a reason: it's meant to appeal to a variety of audiences, from those inside the organization wanting to know where Forward is, to the donating public, institutional funders, its home state's Attorney General, and various watchdog groups.

■ Websites vary in quality, of course, but hopefully you'll be introduced to the organization's leadership (typically a Board of Directors and principal staff), and the programs or activities it's put together to carry out the mission. There'll be presentations of its past and planned accomplishments, and financial reports to show how it's paid for it all and its resulting financial situation, and other features of organizational life.

Tip: Recognize that a nonprofit wants to inform and impress you while staying accountable to all its stakeholders. How well it can do this often depends on whether it can pay for such a site.

Nonprofit missions and their bottom line

An effective nonprofit, we contend, is one that makes progress on its mission — and can show it.

- We say a nonprofit's "bottom line" is defined as "progress made against its mission. "It creates an organizational structure and leadership meant to advance the mission.

- And if a nonprofit can show it's making progress, it can attract supporters.

An effective nonprofit aligns its activities to serve its chosen mission.

- It strives to align its efforts to make its mission come alive and true to the extent possible, given its resources and capacities.

- It creates an organizational structure and leadership meant to advance the mission.

- It raises funds and other resources to be used to advance the mission.

- It designs programs or activities with specific purposes, with the intent to advance the mission by benefiting the individuals, communities, organizations, and/or systems suggested in the mission statement.

  Tip: We hope this book's emphasis on "showing progress against the mission" gives you a point of view you can use.

Nonprofit missions and program strategies—sorting out and reporting out who benefits

Nonprofits typically emphasize one or more of three basic program strategies, each with different intentions:

- **Nonprofit organizations that intend to benefit individuals directly**. The most numerous type of nonprofit, these are the world's original "charities," often rooted in faith–based imperatives "to help," often in emergencies. They offer food, shelter, training, and other assistance so that individuals can regain their footing and move away from the margins of survival.

- **Nonprofits that emphasize benefits to communities directly**. These nonprofits are organized to promote a community's strength, assets, and abilities to improve their community's quality of life. They are organized to create knowledge, wisdom, skills, values, inspiration, beauty, hope, etc. They include organizations that promote education, health, arts & culture, faith, etc, and those that shelter communities from harm and advance their capabilities as a community.

- **Nonprofits that promote upgrades to social systems, so they work better and more fairly, with fewer unfair disparities among different communities**. By systems we include private and public systems and markets – the food systems, the education systems, the health systems, the justice systems, etc., all of which could use some upgrades and all of which could do significantly better if solutions were formulated, tested, and implemented more widely and made to work. Such promotion is within the purview of the nonprofit sector.

We distinguish these three strategies because their success can be gauged and communicated separately for each of three types of beneficiaries, no matter which is the *primary* beneficiary:

- to what extent Individuals benefit

- to what extent Communities benefit

- to what extent Systems perform better

Tip: To make big strides in an arena you care about (Food, Education, Justice, etc.), donate or invest in all three strategies; they each have important roles to play.

Furthermore, nonprofits tend to leave a lot of unreported results on the table, neglecting to take credit for some positive work they do for each of the three beneficiary groups.

Chapter 2
From intentions
to progress:
How nonprofits work

Connecting the dots

Back to sifting through those organizations' requests for support... Ask yourself these nuts and bolts questions:

- Does the organization's mission make sense? Does it seem do–able – or is it so fluffy you can't imagine how they could possibly know what to do? If it makes sense, give them credit.

- Do its activities make sense—as best you can discern them— given what it wants to accomplish? If Yes, you can move it up that Priorities list you're keeping.

- Does it seem to have the horsepower to move ahead? If Yes, move it up some more.

- Does it look like the organization's "intended beneficiaries" (the ones suggested in its mission statement) are actually benefiting in the ways intended, based on what you can glean from its presentation? This is a big one, but if they're showing it, it goes up even higher. For some, this is a make or break question..

- Overall, does its presentation inspire confidence – at some level, enough to give your blessing?

We'll explore these more as we go forward. Each of the questions above is compelling, IMO. Each points to the likelihood this nonprofit plays an important role in saving the world; and with more Yes ratings, the more it's done to achieve real standing and is therefore worthy of support.

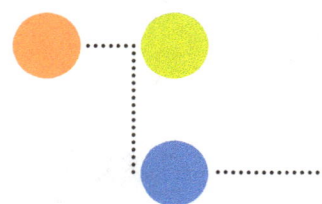

Tip: If I can't see (imagine, understand, sense) how a nonprofit's activities leads to progress on its mission, its request moves lower in my pile of options.

Do they know the way?

We all know there's no "one best way" to address a social issue.

- But does a nonprofit present enough detail (meat, substance) of its approach to give us confidence?

- In the private sector the question is, "Let's see your business model," but the analog doesn't exist in the nonprofit world.

- Closest is when institutional funders ask to see the nonprofit's "theory of action" – the logic or reasoning by which the organization's actions lead to progress on its mission.

  - Unfortunately, constructing such a model is surprisingly difficult. Missions tend to be vague, and the routes to success are not well illuminated.

  - Much of what an organization wants to achieve mission–wise is not really under its control. Still, too many funders ask how the neighborhood's modest food pantry will end world hunger.

  - Most nonprofits hate the logic model exercise. You probably would too. "You want me to explain the logic of my actions? Really?"

Tip: Unless you're OK with accepting the organization's progress on faith — and there's nothing wrong with that — I suggest you support organizations whose efforts align well with the challenge of making progress on its mission.

The essential working parts of a nonprofit organization

To become effective and stay effective, a nonprofit must use a portion of its resources to "build its capacity to make progress on its mission."

We believe these four areas to be essential to the challenge to be effective in the long run:

- **Running the organization**—governance, leadership, staffing, management.

- **Resourcing the organization**—fund raising, financial management, physical and digital resources, communications.

- **Delivering on the mission**—program design, implementation, learning, upgrading, delivering intended benefits to intended beneficiaries.

- **Connecting the organization**—community connections, partnering, joining forces, working with the powers that be.

These are treated separately in the next four pages.

Running the organization

Let's start with the familiar: Leadership and Management. All organizations need ways to run the operation that can advance the mission, to keep the organization on track, and to assure its future.

Typically (and by law in most states), a nonprofit's governance is vested in a Board of Directors, which lays down the basic template for a nonprofit's organization and does its best to assure coherence and accountability.

■ Then there's usually staff, and often volunteers, sometimes advisors and consultants or other people chosen for their authority, wisdom, or connections. Managing, choreographing, organizing all these cats is like herding.

■ That's why there are also rules, guidelines, policies, procedures, secret codes, cultures, and budgets – all intended to keep the organization moving in the right direction.

■ Ideally these are all aligned to support progress against the mission.

There are lots of nonprofit management certificate and advanced degree courses, but I've always been amazed at how little time staff and Board get to look up from the minutiae and crises of daily organizational life to gaze at the bigger picture. They've told me so. "We never get to look at the mission, and how to align our work with it."

Tip: A gift to support special Board or staff meetings ("retreats" and such) to plan or reflect on what the organization has accomplished, and wants to accomplish, how it can draw on the expertise of those who've come before, and especially how it could be take advance of its Strengths and Opportunities coming up, is worth a lot. This sort of gift should be on the list of possibilities for foundations or other charitable funds.

Resourcing the organization

"Resource Development" usually means fundraising, but a nonprofit needs all kinds of resources and skills to develop itself as an organization so it can advance its mission and grow with confidence. As dull as it may sound, it needs:

- A strategy for funding its programs and operations and provide stability and improvement for the next few years.

- A budget, showing where money's going to come from, and what it's going to pay for. Or dog-and-tail like, it can first show what it wants to pay for, and then show where it will get the money.

- A communications strategy that informs stakeholders (the public and others who care) of the organization's mission, special talents, activities, and plans. Oh, and also encourages them to help.

- Equipment, space, expertise, access, blueprints, and the lessons emerging from elsewhere on how to do this work better.

Tip: Gifts of equipment, space, expertise, access, blueprints, software, services, legitimacy, memberships, learning opportunities, next level incentives to grow – all are typically welcome. But better check with them first; no one wants an old printer dropped at their door.

Delivering on the mission

A nonprofit works to advance its mission by creating programs that deliver benefits—at the individual level, the community level, and/or the system level. This is the hard part, but it's what nonprofits are funded to do.

This is what's involved:

- First of all, the organization must be clear about just who it wants to benefit, and in what ways. By doing so, it can better design its programs and activities to accomplish that. Sounds kind of Western and White and Male, I suppose, but if you want to put the ball in the hoop, it's best to know where the hoop is, and what you have to do to get the ball there.

- Then the organization has to design or find a suitable program, perhaps on advice of others who have done it or who can attest to its merit and workability for such an organization. Not any old program will do—it has to deliver the promised benefits! Sounds simple and routine, but it's not, especially since even a good program can take you to places not easily justified to "traditional" stakeholders. New forms of programming need support, testing, and legitimization.

- Most nonprofits conduct more than one program, put together opportunistically, resources permitting. These different programs may have different beneficiaries in mind, or different funders with different expectations and requirements, so making them work in complementary ways over the long haul (ha!) is a challenge.

- Developing strong programs that meet their objectives is itself a real challenge. And to get them to scale is even bigger. It's not that nonprofits don't want to get to scale, wherever that is. It's more that the resources made available are insufficient and inconsistent, and the active or even just inertial forces opposing effectiveness at scale are too strong.

- Last, it's best if nonprofits had the skill and resources to learn from experience so they could make more, better gains and attract more support. Too many nonprofits have little clue how well their programs actually deliver on mission work, and that's usually because they don't have the time, inclination, skill, or money to find out.

Tip: Organizations that seek to evolve ever-stronger programs, often discernable in their materials, rise on my list of priorities. Investing in a nonprofit's ability to learn ought to pay off.

Inter-connecting the organization

To advance its own mission, and to advance the interests of its different community stakeholders, a nonprofit needs:

- Useful and trusting relationships with different segments of the community. A nonprofit, especially an emerging nonprofit, especially those working in areas where structural barriers keep progress down, needs to soften up the territory so that forward progress can be made. It needs help from others, a supportive community especially.

- Skills in creating discussions about local issues that engage local people and help move them closer as potential allies.

- Dexterity in playing the philanthropic game, including partnering with others for mutual benefit, finding ways to connect different organizational assets to make more progress jointly. This could mean breaking down old silos and creating new institutional arrangements up and down the funding supply chain - and getting paid for it!

Because it's so important to make better use of the strengths of existing nonprofits and all the wealth held by institutional funders (which by law have to part with only a pittance each year), we suggest the position of a "Chief Partnership Officer" to expand its mission-focused influence to others, to create stronger networks that can make gains together.

Tip: Funding a new position is a big–ticket item, requiring more than a simple donation.

Becoming more effective should be a goal for any organization

Just as individuals really like to get good with their skills, so should organizations.

- No organization is going to be effective in all these ways all the time, but continuous improvement is needed for long–term viability.

- Different kinds of organizations will talk about "capacity" differently, depending on the nature of their work, their level of development, and the waters they're swimming in – but they're all essential.

There is so much room for growth and improvement it could make your head spin.

For this I blame those institutional funders who, for some reason, pay only for Program Delivery, recognizing its importance but leaving the other three essential areas significantly under–nourished. This creates substantial barriers to meaningful mission progress. It's as if they didn't really want to see effectiveness.

Tip: This gives You plenty of room to make a difference. There is a big need, and many opportunities, to encourage institutional funders to remove barriers to nonprofits' growth and development of mission effectiveness.

Chapter 3
Getting more intentional: Some ideas

Reverse the priorities

Yes, the work is always about upgrading the quality of life of individuals—of people, of real people. But there are many ways to skin a cat.

■ Historically, society has put the most resources into helping individuals one at a time through charities. More recently, especially in the US, the philanthropic sector has put more into supporting communities, and even more recently into advocating for upgrades to social systems.

■ But as suggested, there are many ways to skin a cat. We suggest that by reversing the order of priority we can create more, better progress sooner.

> ■ Let's put *very much more resources* into upgrading systems so they work better ("producing better outcomes") and more equitably ("reducing disparities in these outcomes"). Like this:

> ■ Let's put *much more resources* into supporting communities so they can better support individuals poorly served by the social systems.

> ■ Let's put *more resources* into supporting individuals facing disaster or falling behind.

Tip: Examine your list of solicitations to see where they fall on this continuum, and ask yourself if you want to be more selective of one category or another.

Understanding the work of "social systems"

A "social system" is not a single organization but a mix of organizations, norms, mandates, and practices, that sometimes coordinate and partner, but oftentimes not.

- There are systems of Education, of Health, of Art, of Climate, of Justice, etc – made up of overlapping entities, operating at every political and geographic level, and with different cultures and points of view. Rural is different from urban, "here" is different from "there," and the system's benefits for my culture are typically different, as is shown in endless reams of data, than for yours. Systems are complicated and often mysterious.

- Systems are typically operated and/or governed by public agencies, but they typically also engage nonprofit community organizations, and private or commercial entities, families and individuals – the whole gamut of players that both save and degrade the world. Of this cast of characters, public agencies are certainly the best funded.

- If only we knew how well our systems were operating so we could find clues for upgrading them. If only there were funding that advanced this kind of knowledge of results. We have lots of "problem data" but not so much "solution data." And unfortunately, there's usually resistance to changing systems that people are invested in for various reasons.

- Good news: all systems are created and worked by people – that is, they're human-made, human-powered, and subject to change by humans. Individuals bring imagination and skills to the operation of systems – along with inattention or resistance. If systems are to be upgraded, it'll be by humans.

Tip: Among the solicitations you get, pay attention to the social and political dynamics that likely make things better in the particular arena it's working in. Organizations interested in system change usually provide links to good information.

Nonprofits' role in improving social systems

- It used to be that nonprofits could not engage in "advocacy" or "lobbying," but those rules have been significantly clarified.

- Advocacy – educating the public and policy–making bodies about issues and solutions – is permitted of 501c3 organizations. But lobbying – working to advance specific acts of legislation or to elect specific lawmakers – is generally restricted to 501c4 organizations..

- Nonprofits can educate, advocate, and help advance promising solutions to social problems.

- Nonprofits are the "skunkworks" for testing and advancing promising practices and improved ways of creating opportunities for a better functioning society.

- Anyone can contribute to a nonprofit for such efforts.

Tip: Improving the performance of social systems is too big a job to be left solely to political entities. Organizations that take the larger view and tell me what they're doing within their sphere of influence to push a system's performance are more likely to rise to the top of my Support Now pile.

The value of "advocacy"

Nonprofits engaged in system change try to move solutions along a sequence of somewhat overlapping activities, often called "advocacy."

- Sound the alarm and help a community organize a response.

- Educate the community and its leadership and its representatives to higher authorities and public office.

- Help discover promising solutions that, if implemented, increase the chances of moving a significant system needle.

- Anyone can contribute to any nonprofit for such efforts.

- Encourage policy change and practice inside one's own and others' communities and organizations.

- Encourage new legislation (or enforcement of existing laws) where needed and opportune.

- Promote implementation consistent with the goals of the new rules, monitor its progress, and keep an eye on appropriate system needle(s).

- Insist on upgrades.

Tip: It's unlikely that just one organization can do all of these for even a single issue—again making the case for a Chief Partnership Officer to work the solutions supply chain.

Pushing on the needles of social systems

Nonprofits' role in the craft of upgrading social systems is limited. Nonprofits themselves don't make the rules, or govern, or lobby on behalf of specific candidates to public office. They can, however, educate folks and organizations up and down the line.

- The expression "moving the needle" is part of the vocabulary of system theory.

- It refers to a noticeable change in a meaningful metric that reflects system performance.

- If you're excited about the possibility of meaningful metrics, calm down. Most of the time there are none, or they're way off the mark, or are insufficient in telling the story.

- Still, it's a good exercise to imagine what changes to a system would we like to notice "downstream" from the change. What would there be more of? ... and less of?

- Having these discussions—how to make a system perform better in ways we can observe – is vitally important, and typically not in the budget.

- Figuring out what needles to move—and what actions might make them move—is a big but necessary challenge. Furthermore, moving a needle is most likely a shared endeavor, since needle movement requires several shoulders and the work of several entities. Improving the way this is done is not impossible. One simply must start where one is.

Tip: One doesn't have to be "an advocacy organization" to help a community advance an agenda to improve a system's performance. Any nonprofit can help move things along from its own vantage point and position, but building cooperation among the different entities needed to move a needle is typically not in the "Community Connections" budget if there even is one. Fortunately, anyone can contribute to this effort.

Chapter 4
**Progress counts:
Count progress**

Are nonprofits effective?

If someone were to ask if you personally are doing a good job, if you're effective in whatever role(s) you play in this world, a good answer is probably "Yes and No." Or "Mixed." Or "It's complicated." Right?

Tip: In sifting through requests for support, keep one eye out for how it signifies its own progress – where it's headed, what it's shooting for, what it's proud of, how it "spells success." And whether it's even trying to learn.

- You're doing some things well, other things not so well, and you can see ways to improve. Be honest.

- The same is true for a nonprofit. "Yes and No, Mixed, and It's complicated" apply here too. But we needn't settle for ignorance.

- How effective the organization is can be assessed, in methods ranging from informal to formal.

- Much depends on one's perspective and one's standards. There is no single correct or useful answer. "Yes and No" is almost certainly the best answer, no matter how much money is thrown at conducting a study.

- And whatever the conclusion, the challenge then becomes how to make an organization's efforts better, more effective. An organization can define for itself what a solid "Yes" would look like – what "metrics" or standards it might use—not to prove its effectiveness, but to *improve* its effort, and BTW to educate its supporters.

- Ah, yes, metrics. When people in this arena say metrics, they're trying to sound fancy but usually accept evidence they can understand. Understanding is key.

- How an organization is to be evaluated is typically a matter of choice – usually someone else's. Evaluation is more political and less scientific than usually acknowledged. Any nonprofit organization should be prepared to state and own the standards or criteria by which it wants to be evaluated. Then supporters can pitch in (since self–evaluation isn't usually in the budget), and help it find evidence of its progress.

When it comes to judging effectiveness, one's "point of view" matters

Pretend you're considering a request for support from a nonprofit whose purposes and activities you feel generally supportive of, but you want to know more about its "effectiveness."

■ Now that you're temporarily engaged as an evaluator, you can check the particular point of view (POV) you bring to this task.

■ If you come from the business world you may find it hard to understand that the bottom line for a nonprofit will never be a financial one.

■ And if you come from the science or academic world you might want to see "cause and effect proof" that the activities of the nonprofit "cause" change on some essential outcome or dependent variable. Unfortunately for you, the world is not a controlled laboratory, and therefore scientific standards of proof will never be met. Making things worse, the outcomes most funders are most interested in are far away from the organization's control or even influence.

■ But being a sensible person you look for an alternative, some "noticeable" (inexplicably called "tangible" by some) bits of evidence that together help us understand "the construct of effectiveness" for this kind of organization working at its own level of development in its own time and place and cultural context. And everyone has their own POV.

■ Funders' obsession with "hard data" is a result of excessive testosterone.

■ Just as two eyes are better than one, two bits of evidence are better than one, and five are better than two. Multiple measures (multiple readings from multiple POVs) are needed to understand a complex outcome like "ending hunger."

■ Yes, culture matters, big time. Effectiveness is a construct, requiring multiple lines of evidence, but one's vision of "effectiveness" is very culture-bound, and unless one bothers to understand the culture(s) of the nonprofit's operations, as well as those affecting their progress, you're very likely to impose the values of your culture onto what the nonprofit properly regards as its own domain: its understanding of what it wants to accomplish.

If you've been at this for a while you know that every nonprofit, since money is not the common denominator, thinks differently about the value of its accomplishments. That's why it's important to understand what goes into their own definition, which ought to lead to more satisfying communication.

Tip: If you value progress, support its discovery. Giving a nonprofit the time and resources to fund its own inquiries into its own success is huge.

What can they show?

Here's what you have a right to expect from a nonprofit's presentation of its effectiveness:

- Do you "get" what doing a good job means to them? Do they share what mission-related accomplishments they feel good about at the end of the proverbial day?

- Does its description of activities and accomplishments tell us (even between the lines) what they hope happens for their intended beneficiaries as a fairly immediate consequence (forget about long–term) of their connection to the program?

- Do they spend resources—effort, time, money—in search of signs that these intended benefits are happening? For example, do they deploy volunteers to "stalk the wild outcome," see what's happening in the audience, or on the street, or in next week's meeting, or wherever the program meets its people?

- Do they occasionally interview (with focus groups and/or questionnaires) those they've tried to benefit, with an eye to learning what's working and how to improve?

- Is there a record or documentation of beneficiaries benefiting? If not through formal inquiries, how about some good artifacts? Meeting notes, perhaps, or event programs? Any good stories or photos or maps or dances or images on the side of a building or a bar napkin? Perhaps a scrapbook of all the above? (I recommend this.)

For those of you thinking this isn't real science, I say it is real empiricism, which is the root of all science. We're asking for observable evidence—evidence that this dog hunts, these seeds grow, these labors bear fruit, this program works as advertised. Show me.

Bottom line: When you align its presentation alongside its mission statement, can you reasonably conclude this nonprofit is making progress?

Tip: It's possible the nonprofit's Development Officer keeps track of success stories, however defined. It's also possible that the just-right donation could help them develop a more thorough, systematic, or meaningful presentation. As any nonprofit will tell you, it takes money to develop this kind of evidence and work it into a compelling presentation.

The art of making choices—vetting priorities

An organization of people working towards a worthwhile common goal is a thing of beauty—when it's actually working. How might we know?

- "Due diligence" as it's known in the private sector – the art of appraising a private enterprise's worthiness for investment – is well-developed, focusing on financial and management considerations.

- But accepted standards for an appraisal of a nonprofit's potential for making good on its mission? They don't exist. Showing low overhead costs only means they have a good accountant. What it pays its leadership might be more meaningful.

By now you shouldn't be surprised to see my three big basic questions for sorting requests into Higher vs Lower Priorities:

- Do the organization's activities make sense, given its stated purposes or mission? If not, is it trying to learn how to do it better?

- Does the organization have the muscle – the skills, resources, commitment – to make progress on its mission? If not, does it seem to know what it takes to gain strength?

- Bottom line: Can it show progress – a collection of different indications – bits of data or evidence that suggest it's making progress on the mission? If not, are they working on it?

Tip: Try using these three questions to sort your priorities from High to Low. Is it better than nothing?

What the world needs now is ... signs of progress!

Apologies to Burt Bacharach. Though he makes a good point.

The world isn't going to be saved overnight, or in a year, or with the one just-right program or policy.

It's people that will save the world, donating, investing, and serving in a smart accumulation of efforts that together make progress against specific meritorious goals.

And then, of course, there's Sisyphus, who also makes a good point. And Don Quixote.

Tip: "Do not get lost in a sea of despair. Be hopeful, be optimistic. Our struggle is not the struggle of a day, a week, a month, or a year. It is the struggle of a lifetime."

-Rep. John Lewis

The art and science of making choices

As you look over the possibilities—the list of nonprofits asking for your financial support—you wonder how to choose among them.

- In the end, of course, it's your choice, and you don't have to justify it to anyone. One's choice is typically personally motivated. A gift is a gift, and a gift is usually personal.

- Do you give with your head, looking only at the facts? Or do you give with your heart, looking inside for guidance? I suggest both, and there's a continuum...

The "heart-to-head continuum" of decision-making

- Heart: Personally identifying with the mission and sensing your own sympathy, empathy, prayers, hope, and best wishes for the organization.

- Head: Personally identifying with the mission and being reasonably assured that it knows what it's doing, that its activities make sense, and that it has the organizational "capacity" to take it where it wants to go.

- Both: Personally identifying with the mission and seeing evidence, some stronger than others, that adds up to a judgment, admittedly shaky, that the organization is making progress against its mission – delivering on its promise to its intended beneficiaries – and you wish it well.

Tip: Pick an area, any area – Arts, Justice, Food – learn what you can about the issues, about the organizations playing useful roles close to home and farther away. Learn what factors advance (and impede) constructive change. School yourself on the possibilities. Scan your mail and the internet for examples and opportunities.

Chapter 5
Next-level effectiveness: Up your game

Can we (institutional funders and the rest of us) all just get along?

Can we—those who show our care by doing the real work, and those who show our care by providing support – get on the same page with "what progress looks like" in different critical arenas? Right now, we're not.

Right now, too many institutional funders and many individuals are asking the wrong questions, and their process can be burdensome and thoughtless. Funders can ask for the darndest things. On that list:

- Proof that the nonprofit's program works, as determined by double–blind randomly assigned comparison, per Science.

- Evidence that an organization's efforts are in fact saving the world, expressed in quantitative terms.

- Budgetary data showing how much is spent on "program vs. administration." This could make sense if the data weren't so easily rigged.

- Impact per dollar. It's embarrassing how much contemporary society believes that money is the only real signifier of value. How much good something does is not, at root, a financial question.

To me, an organization that can adequately show evidence it is making progress against its stated mission is worthy of further investment. Period.

We're not asking for proof of anything, we're asking for evidence of something. What nonprofits show of their effectiveness doesn't have to be earth-shaking or "transformative," but it must be something, even a scrapbook showing a collection of scraps that, when taken together spells "success so far," or "progress." Nonprofits are able to teach us what's important to them. We'll know when we think and/or feel they're on to something worth further support.

Tip: Of course, an organization asking for support should also be able to show it's legit in the eyes of the law, and operating in ways a CPA can put their name to. Anyone can explore this on its website, or its entry in Guidestar.org (specialized in reporting on US nonprofits), or the state's Attorney General (which is charged with oversight of the state's registered nonprofits) or less formally the state's Association of Nonprofit Organizations (which may assist both healthy and unhealthy nonprofits).

Up your game

**Moi, when it comes to saving the world,
I'm feeling a sense of urgency.**

- Too many life-sustaining systems are dysfunctional or performing way below what's needed.

- Too many people and communities are falling through the cracks, barely getting what's needed for survival.

What can we do?

- At the least, we can choose to pay more attention. And look for opportunities to support next-level effectiveness.

- Notice the signs of disrepair, yes, but also the signs of life, energy, hope, re—building, and building anew. Show respect for the possibilities.

- Help build on the strengths and assets of individuals and communities.

- Remember: Generosity is a good thing.

Tip: Make a plan. Focus on an area, a theme, a vision of what you'd like to see happen, something you'd like to help happen. Create a "giving circle" if you don't want to do this alone.

Learn more about an issue that interests you

Pick a theme, any theme, just for the purpose of learning more about it.

- The internet is a crazy useful tool for just this purpose. Explore breaking down traditional silos and changing lanes. In the browser's search bar, just type in "Food and Criminal Justice Reform," *et voila*! On the first page of results is an amazing variety of ways in to this choice subject. Or try "Climate and Film." Just try it.

- If you're not intrigued enough to click through on at least three of those choice leads, I'll give you double your money back on whatever you paid for this chapter.

- And maybe saving the world just isn't your thing right now. Maybe you'll be back later.

Tip: But if you did click through a few of these, and felt your interest engaged, your blood rising, your money app opening, your calendar revealing a time to inquire personally with someone you know of, some wish to show support... then please continue.

Find or create opportunities for building strengths

All people, communities, and organizations, have strengths (despite their weaknesses or needs).

The Western world has been conditioned to look at needs rather than strengths, especially in the world of philanthropy borne from the imperative to "help those less fortunate."

But one has a choice in the lens one uses to look at those "less fortunate."

- You can look at individuals, communities and their organizations, and see their glass as half empty, as needy. Seeing needs may encourage charity, but it doesn't encourage growth.

- On the other hand, you can see the glass as half full. Seeing it as half full encourages you to look for opportunities for growth, where they can build on strengths to become stronger.

- You can even look at both, and look for evidence of change through each lens: a) reduction of unfavorable events, and b) increase of favorable events.

- Unfortunately, those asking for help are too often coming from Need, and not often enough coming from Strength, making it difficult for them to attract "strength money."

Tip: Invest in further strengthening. Fill those glasses! The world needs and deserves stronger individuals, communities, and organizations that support them.

What's a good gift?

The value of a gift is usually reckoned better by the receiver than the giver. You can be sure a gift of money won't be turned down. But a gift of money that has strings attached may not be much of a gift.

These kinds of financial gifts are most appreciated:

- A gift of money in support of an organization's general operations.

- A gift of money in support of a specific project if it covers the associated organizational costs.

- A gift of money in support of a project if it allows the organization to become stronger in one or more of the ways described in the section on useful organizational muscles.

To be saved, the world needs gifts that help grow strengths. This could mean gifts of these kinds:

- Gifts that help nonprofits find and partner with other nonprofits with aligned interests in ways that add value to both their efforts.

- Gifts that help nonprofits move solutions from one stage to the next.

- Gifts that help nonprofits use more different tools for growing their mission–related work.

- Gifts that help nonprofits gain further understanding of their progress, and how to make further progress.

What's not a good gift?

Remember, a gift is not a contract.

■ You may hope that something good happens through your gift, but a hope is not a promise and it's certainly not guaranteed. There are so many things that can keep a good organization from actualizing its potential. As a mentor told me, "There can be many a slip between the cup and the lip."

■ Donating to a nonprofit does not – legally can not – result in a financial return to you, whether in cash or in services. Fortunately, there are many "returns on your investment" that are not financial. Seeing a cause you care about come closer to its vision is one of those.

Give with your head *and* your heart

We introduced the "head–heart" continuum of decision–making earlier. Here it relates to where an appeal for your support grabs you, and whether to follow your heart or your head.

- You can give with your heart—appeals that align with values you embrace, that make you say "Awww," that make you want to reach for the Donate button with little further thought. Not that there's anything wrong with that.

- You can give with your head—appeals showing numbers, showing tables, charts, infographics, and other cool stuff meant to have you conclude they must know what they're doing. Maybe so.

- You can give with your head and your heart. Real intelligence seeks to align values with evidence presented in ways you can trust.

And who knows what Artificial Intelligence will bring to this arena: hopefully some tools to align sufficient resources to constructive efforts, build pathways to progress, bend the trend lines, and save the world.

Thanks for reading and considering this!

Steven E. Mayer, Ph.D.

Extra credit

The following posts, easily found on the "Writings" page of the website for the Effective Communities Project, support many of the themes in this book. You can find the site at *https://EffectiveCommunities.com*.

Re Chapter 1 – The Work of Nonprofit Organizations

- Why Becoming More Like a Business Is Not the Solution for Nonprofits
- Philanthropic Effectiveness: What Making a Difference Really Means
- Nonprofit Development and Evaluation: The Untold Story of Who Benefits from Nonprofit Programs

Re Chapter 2 – How Nonprofits Work

- How Nonprofits Are Set-up To Fail: Ghosts from Our Pre-Colonial Past
- The Assets Model of Community Development
- What is a Disadvantaged Group?

Re Chapter 3 – Getting More Intentional

- Use Advocacy to Promote Social Change
- Saving the Babies: Looking Upstream for Solutions
- Evaluation Court: A Mock Trial to Judge Program Effectiveness

Re Chapter 4 – Progress Counts – Count Progress

- The Choices We Make as Evaluators: You Gotta Serve Somebody
- Looking for Evidence of Success? Follow the Action
- Wanted: Better Evaluation Practices for a Better Philanthropy

Re Chapter 5 – Next Level Effectiveness

- Good Trouble, Necessary Trouble
- Building Community Capacity: The Potential of Community Foundations
- Happy Birthday, America!